Published in 2012 by Helen Exley Giftbooks
in Great Britain. Edited by Helen Exley © Helen Exley Creative Ltd
2012. Illustrations by Angela Kerr © Helen Exley Creative Ltd
2012. Design, illustration selection and arrangement © Helen
Exley Creative Ltd 2012. The moral right of the author has been
asserted.

The publishers are grateful for permission to reproduce copyright
material. Whilst every reasonable effort has been made to trace
copyright holders, the publishers would be pleased to hear from
any not here acknowledged.
Words by Pam Brown © Helen Exley Creative Ltd 2012.

12 11 10 9 8 7 6 5 4 3 2 1

ISBN: 978-1-84634-681-1

Helen Exley Giftbooks,
16 Chalk Hill, Watford, Herts,
WD19 4BG, UK.

www.helenexleygiftbooks.com

Follow us on and

Doing
The Right Thing
The foundation of a happy life

EDITED BY HELEN EXLEY
ILLUSTRATIONS BY ANGELA KERR

A HELEN EXLEY GIFTBOOK

We must use time
creatively,
and forever realise
that the time is always
ripe to do right.

NELSON ROLIHLAHLA
MANDELA B. 1918

Live in the present,
do all the things
that need to be done.
Do all the good you can
each day.
The future will unfold.

PEACE PILGRIM

I expect to pass through
life but once.
If therefore, there be
any kindness I can show,
or any good thing
I can do to any fellow being,
let me do it now,
and not defer or neglect it,
as I shall not pass
this way again.

WILLIAM PENN
1644 – 1718

*To be a good,
warm-hearted person
is definitely
the root of peace,
happiness,
and everything good.*

DALAI LAMA B. 1935

W e must not,
in trying to think about
how we can make
a big difference,
ignore the small daily
differences we can make
which, over time,
add up to big differences
that we often
cannot foresee.

MARIAN WRIGHT EDELMAN
B. 1939

*The best portion
of a good man's life – his little,
nameless, unremembered acts
of kindness and of love.*

WILLIAM WORDSWORTH
1770 – 1850

A cynic...
is overcome by the goodness
of little people.

PAM BROWN B. 1928

All the beautiful
sentiments
in the world
weigh less than
a single
lovely action.

JAMES RUSSELL LOWELL
1819 – 1891

To laugh often and much;
to win the respect of
intelligent people and
the affection of children;
to earn the appreciation of
honest critics and endure
the betrayal of false friends.
To appreciate beauty;
to find the best in others;
to leave the world a bit better
whether by a healthy child,

a garden patch or a
redeemed social condition;
to know that even one life
has breathed easier
because you have lived.
This is to have succeeded.

RALPH WALDO EMERSON
1803 – 1882

The work an unknown
good individual has done
is like a vein of water flowing
hidden underground, secretly
making the ground green.

THOMAS CARLYLE
1795 – 1881

A PERSON'S TRUE WEALTH
IS THE GOOD HE OR SHE
DOES IN THE WORLD.

MOHAMMED

A charitable person
enjoys an abundant life;
a greedy person is
always poor.

WANG FANZHI

There is no
beautifier
of complexion,
or form,
or behavior, like
the wish to scatter
joy and not
pain around us.

RALPH WALDO EMERSON
1803 – 1882

*May something
you do or say
make all the difference
to someone's life.*

PAM BROWN B. 1928

NEVER UNDERESTIMATE THE POWER OF A SIMPLE GOOD ACT.

FR. BRIAN D'ARCY B. 1945

If there be righteousness
in the heart,
there will be beauty
in the character.
If there be beauty in
the character, there will
be harmony in the home.
If there be harmony
in the home, there will
be order in the nation.
If there be order in the
nation, there will be peace
in the world.

CONFUCIUS 551 – 479 B.C.

B<small>E</small> GOOD
TO YOURSELF,
B<small>E</small> EXCELLENT
TO OTHERS,
AND
D<small>O</small> EVERYTHING
WITH LOVE.

JOHN WOLF

Love for mankind is a vast enterprise – but it has good beginnings in smiles, in holding open doors, in giving a hand with push chairs, in giving up one's seat. Consideration and respect lighten the world.

PAM BROWN B. 1928

Life is made up,
for the most part, not of great
occasions, but of small
everyday moments, it is
the giving to those moments
their greatest amount
of peace, pleasantness,
and security, that contributes
most to the sum of
human good. Be peaceable.
Be cheerful. Be true.

LEIGH HUNT 1784 – 1859

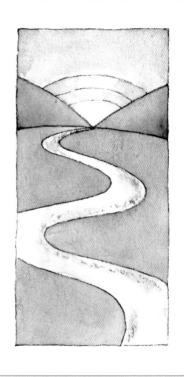

This is what you shall do:
Love the earth and sun
and the animals,
despise riches, give alms
to everyone
that asks, stand up
for the stupid and crazy,
devote your income
and labor to others,
hate tyrants.

WALT WHITMAN
1819 – 1892

We can never
give up the belief
that the good guys
always win.
And that we are
the good guys.

FAITH POPCORN

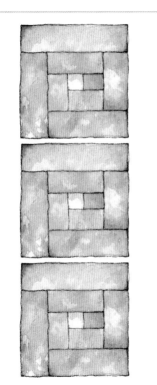

*I have known
what happiness is,
for I have
done good work.*

ROBERT LOUIS STEVENSON
1850 – 1894

The only real satisfaction
there is, is to be growing up
inwardly all the time,
becoming more just, true,
generous, simple, manly,
womanly, kind, active.

JAMES FREEMAN CLARKE
1810 – 1888

Perhaps our only refu

is in t

goodness in each other.

PAM BROWN B. 1928

In each human
heart's core
there is a divine essence.
The evils which appear
on the surface
are not found in the depths.
We must find a way
to penetrate the depth
of each human heart
and to draw
out the goodness
with which it is filled.

VINOBA BHAVE
1894 – 1982

Everyone IS BORN GOOD.

CONFUCIUS 551 – 479 B.C.

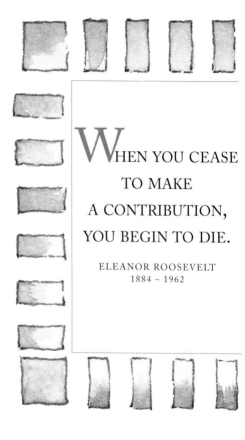

WHEN YOU CEASE TO MAKE A CONTRIBUTION, YOU BEGIN TO DIE.

ELEANOR ROOSEVELT
1884 – 1962

*E*xecute
every act of thy life
as though
it were thy last.

MARCUS AURELIUS
121 – 180

Goodness is something
so simple;
always live for others,
never to seek one's own
advantage.

DAG HAMMARSKJÖLD
1905 – 1961

In the pursuit of happiness
half the world is on
the wrong scent.
They think it consists
in having and getting,
and in being served by others.
Happiness is really found
in giving and in serving others.

HENRY DRUMMOND
1851 – 1897

*Wish not
so much to live long
as to live well.*

BENJAMIN FRANKLIN
1706 – 1790

Love all,
trust a few,
Do wrong
to none.

WILLIAM SHAKESPEARE
1564 – 1616

Waste
NO MORE TIME
ARGUING WHAT
A GOOD PERSON
SHOULD BE.
Be one.

MARCUS AURELIUS
121 – 180

*There is within each of us
a potential for goodness beyond
our imagining; for giving
which seeks no reward; for
listening without judgement;
for loving unconditionally.*

ELISABETH KÜBLER-ROSS
1926 – 2004

There is goodness in
everything. Our job is to
find it. In every setback there
is the key to success.
Our challenge is to find it.
In every person,
the best is there.
It's up to us to discover it!

SOLOMON IBN GABIROL

Have confidence in
yourself to do what
you think is right.
Fear not what others
might say. Press ahead
with determination
and dignity.

DEREK DOBSON

Make all you can,
save all you can,
give all you can.

WALT WHITMAN
1819 – 1892

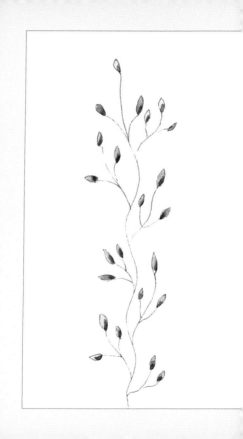

Whatever the world
may say or do, my part
is to keep myself good;
just as a gold piece,
or an emerald, or
a purple robe insists
perpetually,
"Whatever the world
may say or do, my part
is to remain an emerald
and keep my colour true."

MARCUS AURELIUS
121 – 180

STAND AT
THE CROSSROADS,
AND LOOK,
AND ASK FOR
THE ANCIENT PATHS,
WHERE THE GOOD
WAY LIES,
AND WALK IN IT.

JEREMIAH 6:16

To awaken each morning
with a smile brightening my face;
to greet the day with
reverence for the opportunities
it contains; to approach
my work with a clean mind;
to hold ever before me,
even in the doing of little things,
the ultimate purpose toward
which I am working;
to meet men and women
with laughter on my lips
and love in my
heart; to be gentle, kind,

and courteous through
all the hours; to approach
the night with weariness
that ever woos sleep and the joy
that comes from work
well done – this is how
I desire to waste wisely my days.

THOMAS DEKKER
C.1570 – 1632

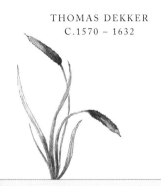

Ten Thousand Miles

is really nothing
if one is
seeking for
the truth.

MEI YAOCHENG

Be sincere
in your thoughts,
Be pure in your
feelings. You will
not have to run after
happiness.
Happiness will
run after you.

SRI CHINMOY
1931 – 2007

Speak or act with
a pure mind, and
happiness will follow
you as your
shadow, unshakable.

THE BUDDHA
C.563 – 483 B.C.

Once you have said,
"It is enough,"
you are lost.
Keep adding,
keep walking,
keep advancing;
do not stop,
do not turn back,
do not turn from
the straight road.

ST. AUGUSTINE 354 – 430

THE TIME IS ALWAYS RIGHT TO DO WHAT IS RIGHT.

MARTIN LUTHER KING JR
1929 – 1968

*B*e more concerned
with your character
than your reputation,
because your character
is what you really are,
while your reputation
is merely what
others think you are.

JOHN WOODEN

The promised land may be many things to many people. For some it is perfect health and for others freedom from hunger or fear, or discrimination, or injustice. But perhaps on the deepest level the promised land is the same for us all, the capacity to know and live by the innate goodness in us, to serve and belong to one another and to life.

RACHEL NAOMI REMEN

Every good that you do,
every good that you say,
every good thought
you think, vibrates on
and on and never ceases.
The evil remains only until
it is overcome by good,
but the good remains forever...

PEACE PILGRIM

Strive with all
the energy you have.
Ignore criticism from those
who cannot see.
Have the strength to pursue
your vision. And in the end
you will achieve your goal.
For what is right
will succeed. It is then
that others will learn
from what you have done,
and make
it all worthwhile.

DEREK DOBSON

It seems to me that
we can never give up
longing and wishing while
we are thoroughly alive.
There are certain things
we feel to be beautiful
and good, and we must
hunger after them.

GEORGE ELIOT,
(MARY ANN EVANS)
1819 – 1880

And do not change.
Do not divert your love
from visible things.
But go on loving
what is good, simple
and ordinary; animals
and things and flowers,
and keep the balance true.

RAINER MARIA RILKE
1875 – 1926

Our readers have bought more than 80 million copies of our works in forty five languages. Helen spares no expense in making sure that each book is as thoughtful and meaningful as it is possible to create. With infinite care, Helen has researched the words for this series over decades. If you have found this book valuable please tell others!

If you love this book…

… you will probably want to know how to find other HELEN EXLEY® products like it. They're all listed on

www.helenexley.com